THE PERFECT
Pâté

Bernice Hurst

Illustrations
by Ronald Hurst

HAMLYN

Published 1985 by Hamlyn Publishing,
a division of The Hamlyn Publishing Group Ltd,
Bridge House, 69 London Road,
Twickenham, Middlesex

© Elvendon Press 1979, 1985

ISBN 0 600 32526 1

Printed in Italy

CONTENTS

Pâté is not difficult to make. The ingredients are easily obtainable and the variations infinite. The only equipment which is essential is a good, sharp knife and a mincer, either hand or electric. A liquidiser helps, but you can manage just as well with a sieve and a strong arm. Any pan or ovenproof dish can be used.

Meat pâtés are combinations of minced or chopped liver, poultry and game with a certain amount of fat included to help retain the flavours and juices. This, of course, is the essence of pâté – full flavour and tender, moist consistency. There are certain other steps which ensure that end. Herbs, wines and spirits are added to enhance the flavour of the meats. Cooking is frequently done in a bain marie, i.e. roasting pan half filled with water, to ensure that the pâté does not dry out. When cooling, the pâté can be compressed with heavy weights to make slicing simpler. It can then be served directly from the dish in which it was cooked, or easily turned out. If turned out, it can be glazed with gelatin or wrapped in pastry.

Most of the pâtés in this book use fairly large quantities of ingredients. Pâtés keep very well – they can be sealed with lard or clarified butter and kept for up to a month in a cool place. Once they are cut, they should keep for a week or more in the refrigerator. The quantities given will serve up to twenty, depending on whether they are used as starters or meals. Most of the recipes can be halved quite easily, or the full quantity can be made in two pans, one for eating immediately and the other for keeping. Cooking times are obviously approximate, depending on the depth of the pan being used. To test whether the pâté is cooked, insert a skewer. It will come out clean if the pâté is ready. The juices will also be clear and yellow.

To test for seasoning, a small spoonful of the raw mixture can be sautéed for a few minutes in a bit of butter. This is advisable as there is little you can do once the pâté is cooked.

If your taste runs to smooth pâtés, either continue mincing the ingredients until they are perfectly smooth, or liquidise or sieve them.

Fat of some kind should be used to line the pan to ensure the pâté does not dry out. Although bacon rashers, pork fat and salt pork have been specified for each recipe, these are interchangeable according to taste. The fat can be put either at the bottom of the pan or in strips on top of the pâté mixture. Either way, it is not meant to be eaten and can be removed after cooking.

Non-meat pâtés are puréed mixtures of vegetables or fish. They tend to be very light and make a delicious alternative to the traditional meat-liver mixtures. They are usually quicker to make as well since they do not require long baking. A few hours to chill the dish is usually sufficient.

Each of the recipes given here has been tested. That is not to say, however, that you must follow them exactly. If you want more or less of an ingredient, fine. If you'd rather substitute something else, fine. If you want to add a few mushrooms, nuts, olives, peppercorns or anything else that takes your fancy, fine. Pâtés are like that. Nearly every restaurant has its own Pâté Maison – there is no reason why every home should not have its own Perfect Pâté.

PÂTÉ DE CAMPAGNE (1)

Pâté de Campagne – Country Pâté – is a very loose title, like Pâté Maison. In France, each area of the country, and even individual homes, have their own special recipes.

6-8 rashers streaky bacon
350 g/12 oz calf's liver
675 g/1½ lb pie veal
1 large onion
2 cloves garlic, crushed
1 tbsp tomato purée

½ tsp sage
½ tsp oregano
salt and pepper
100 g/4 oz butter, melted
150 ml/¼ pint red wine
1 bay leaf

Line baking dish with bacon.

Mince liver, veal and onion. Add garlic, tomato purée, seasoning, butter and wine. Mix well. Turn into baking dish and place bay leaf on top.

Cover with foil and bake 2 hours at 180C/350F/gas 4. Place a heavy weight on the pâté while it is cooling.

Chill before serving.

PÂTÉ DE CAMPAGNE (2)

6-8 rashers streaky bacon
225 g/8 oz pie veal, cut
  in strips
225 g/8 oz pig's liver
225 g/8 oz pork fat
225 g/8 oz sausage meat
1 small onion

1 clove garlic
2 hardboiled eggs, chopped
½ tsp parsley
½ tsp marjoram
½ tsp thyme
salt and pepper
1 bay leaf

Line baking dish with bacon rashers.

Mince liver, pork fat, onion and garlic. Add sausage meat, eggs and seasoning. Mix well.

Spread half of liver mixture over bacon in baking dish. Arrange strips of veal on top. Cover with remaining liver mixture and place bay leaf in centre.

Cover the pan with foil, place in a larger pan with enough hot water to go halfway up sides of pâté dish. Bake 1 hour at 180C/350F/gas 4.

Cool, then chill before serving.

PÂTÉ DE CAMPAGNE (3)

4-6 rashers streaky bacon
225 g/8 oz pie veal, minced
225 g/8 oz sausage meat
100 g/4 oz chicken liver, chopped
2 cloves garlic, finely chopped
1 tsp juniper berries, crushed
½ tsp sage
½ tsp thyme
pinch ground mace
salt and pepper
1 tbsp dry sherry
1 bay leaf

Line baking dish with bacon rashers.

Combine veal, sausage meat, sherry, garlic and seasoning. Mix well.

Turn half of meat mixture into baking dish. Arrange pieces of liver on top and cover with remaining meat. Place bay leaf in centre. Cover the dish with foil and bake 1¾ hours at 180C/350F/gas 4. Place a heavy weight on the pâté while it is cooling.

Chill before serving.

CHICKEN LIVER PÂTÉ (1)

Definitely a dinner party dish, this first classic pâté is very smooth, strong and rich. It will go a long way as portions must be small. The second version is somewhat lighter with the chicken livers complemented by a wine flavoured gelatin.

450 g/1 lb chicken liver	½ tsp parsley
150 g/5 oz butter	½ tsp marjoram
salt and pepper	½ tsp thyme
1 clove garlic, crushed	50 ml/2 fl oz dry sherry
pinch mixed spice	2 tbsp brandy

Gently fry liver in 50 g/2 oz butter until just firm. Add garlic and seasoning. Continue cooking until well blended, 1-2 minutes. Remove from the cooker and stir in sherry and brandy.

Turn liver into liquidiser and blend until smooth. Add 75 g/3 oz softened butter. Mix well. Turn into serving dish. Chill before serving.

An optional variation would be to add 2 beaten eggs to the liver mixture while it is still cooking and allow them to set before liquidising. In this case, the sherry and brandy can be added at the same time as the softened butter.

CHICKEN LIVER PÂTÉ (2)

6-8 rashers streaky bacon
900 g/2 lb chicken liver
4 tbsp butter
1 small onion, chopped
½ tsp oregano
½ tsp marjoram
salt and pepper
4 tbsp brandy

4½ tbsp single cream
4 eggs
1 bay leaf
Glaze
2 tsp unflavoured gelatin
175 ml/6 fl oz dry white wine
½ tsp oregano
½ tsp parsley

Line pan with bacon rashers, placing bay leaf in the centre.

Gently fry onions in soft butter until soft. Add herbs and liver and cook 5 minutes longer. Turn into liquidiser, add brandy, cream and eggs. Blend until smooth. Season with salt and pepper.

Turn into pan, place in larger pan of hot water. Bake 1 hour at 200C/400F/gas 6. Cool then chill overnight. Turn onto plate, remove bacon rashers and bay leaf. Smooth surface and glaze. Allow to set before serving.

TO MAKE GLAZE

Dissolve gelatin in 50 ml/2 fl oz water in small bowl over pan of hot water. Add wine and herbs. Transfer bowl to larger bowl, full of ice. Stir until thickened. Glaze pâté.

CHICKEN LIVER AND PORK PÂTÉ

*Chicken liver and pork mingle well in this coarse, juicy pâté.
As with most pâtés, it is best kept overnight before serving – this
allows the herbs and liquors to permeate the meat mixture.*

6-8 rashers streaky bacon
450 g/1 lb chicken liver
225 g/8 oz belly pork
225 g/8 oz lean pork
2 tbsp red wine
2 tbsp sweet sherry

1 clove garlic, crushed
½ tsp thyme
pinch ground mace
salt and pepper
1 bay leaf

Coarsely mince liver and pork. Add wine, sherry and
seasoning. Mix well. Allow to marinate overnight.

Line baking dish with bacon rashers.

Turn mixture into pan and place bay leaf in centre. Cover
the pan with foil, place in a larger pan with enough hot water
to go halfway up sides of pâté dish. Bake 1¾ hours at 180C/
350F/gas 4.

Chill before serving.

CHOPPED LIVER

A traditional Jewish recipe which is at its best when made with chicken liver and chicken fat.

3 tbsp chicken fat, cut into small pieces
1 tbsp onion, finely chopped

225 g/8 oz chicken liver
1 medium onion, chopped
2 hardboiled eggs
½ tsp salt

First slowly cook the chicken fat and 1 tbsp onion. When the fat is melted and the remaining "bits" are very brown and crispy, drain. Reserve onions and use the fat for cooking the liver and remaining onion.

Cool liver slightly then chop finely or mince along with the fried onion and eggs. Add salt, crispy bits of onion and chicken fat and enough liquid chicken fat to bind.

Chill before serving.

DANISH PÂTÉ

Although pâté is generally considered a speciality of France, many other countries have their own delicious versions. The Danish approach is quite different, blending liver, bacon and anchovies with a white sauce to create a truly appetising spread.

6-8 rashers streaky bacon
450 g/1 lb pig's liver
175 g/6 oz unsmoked fat back bacon
6 anchovy fillets
salt and pepper
pinch ground allspice
pinch ground nutmeg

pinch ground cloves
1 egg, beaten
300 ml/½ pint milk
1 onion
1 bay leaf
25 g/1 oz butter
25 g/1 oz plain flour

Line baking dish with bacon.

Slowly bring milk, onion and bay leaf to the boil. Cover and allow to infuse for 15 minutes. Strain before using.

Mince liver, bacon and anchovies finely. It may be necessary to put them through the mincer a second time to get a very smooth mixture. Add seasoning and mix well.

Make a white sauce by stirring the flour into the melted butter and gradually adding the hot milk. Stir until thickened. Add the sauce and beaten egg to the liver mixture. Blend well. Turn into baking dish. Cover with foil, place in a larger pan with enough hot water to go halfway up sides of pâté dish. Bake 2 hours at 160C/325F/gas 3. Place a heavy weight on the pâté while it is cooling.

ng.

PORK PÂTÉ WITH MUSHROOMS

A flavoursome combination of liver, veal and ham. This pâté is made particularly smooth by liquidising the meat mixture after it has been minced then adding bits of mushroom.

450 g/1 lb pig's liver	2 tbsp parsley
thin slices of pork fat	1 small onion, chopped
225 g/8 oz pie veal	25 g/1 oz lard
225 g/8 oz fatty ham	salt and pepper
175 g/6 oz breadcrumbs	½ tsp sage
50 ml/2 fl oz milk	½ tsp basil
2 eggs, beaten	50 g/2 oz mushrooms, chopped
4 tbsp brandy	1 bay leaf

Line baking dish with pork fat.

Mince liver, veal and ham finely. Soak the breadcrumbs in milk until soft. Gently cook the onion in melted lard until soft. Add breadcrumbs, onion, brandy, eggs and seasoning to meat mixture. Turn into liquidiser and blend until smooth. Soften mushrooms in 15 g/½ oz butter and fold into mixture. Turn into baking dish and place bay leaf in centre. Cover the pan with foil, place in a larger pan with enough hot water to go halfway up sides of pâté dish. Bake 1½ hours at 160C/325F/gas 3.

Chill before serving.

PÂTÉ EN CROÛTE

The combination of liver and bacon imparts its flavour to the pastry, making a delicious pâté which is also an attractive centrepiece. The procedure of encasing pâté in pastry can be followed with any other recipe equally well.

10 streaky bacon rashers	4 tbsp sherry
450 g/1 lb piece of streaky bacon	1 tsp nutmeg
2 onions	½ tsp mixed herbs
225 g/8 oz chicken liver	1 tsp salt
2 tbsp plain flour	8 oz puff pastry
4 tbsp milk	beaten egg to glaze
2 eggs	

Bring piece of bacon to boil in cold water. When it is cooked, cool slightly then skin and put through mincer twice, adding the liver and onion the second time. Mix thoroughly with the flour, eggs, milk, sherry, nutmeg, salt and herbs.

Line baking pan with the streaky rashers. Smooth pâté mixture into pan. Bake 50 minutes at 180C/350F/gas 4. Cool. Turn onto plate, remove bacon and smooth surface.

Roll pastry out thinly, place pâté in centre and fold edges over, sealing with the beaten egg. Use remaining egg to glaze surface. Bake in hot oven, 200C/400F/gas 6, until golden brown. Serve cold.

PÂTÉ PASTIES

An unusual and successful way of presenting a spicy, crumbly mixture of pre-cooked ingredients. Excellent when warm. The pastry is flaky and puffs up when baked.

Pastry
175 g/6 oz plain flour
¼ tsp salt
100 g/4 oz margarine
6-8 tbsp top of milk (single cream)
Filling
4 rashers streaky bacon
3 chicken livers
½ tsp salt
1 hardboiled egg
½ tsp curry powder
½ tsp made up mustard
¼ tsp pepper
pinch paprika
2 tbsp parsley
¾ tsp salt
1 egg, beaten

Rub margarine into combined salt and flour, add enough cream to bind into dough. Chill while preparing filling.

Fry bacon until crisp. Drain, reserving fat. Use 2 tbsp bacon fat to brown liver. Add ½ tsp salt and simmer for 5 minutes. Drain liver, chop along with hardboiled egg and bacon. Add seasoning, remaining salt and 2 tsp bacon fat. Mix well and chill for ½ hour.

Roll dough thinly and cut into 6-cm/2½-in rounds. Put ½ tsp liver mixture onto each round, brush edges with beaten egg and seal.

When the pasties are ready for baking, brush surface with beaten egg. Bake 20-25 minutes at 220C/425F/gas 7.

LIVER PÂTÉ WITH HAZELNUTS

This recipe and Paprikáspastétom on the opposite page were collected by Sheila Hutchins for her excellent book 'Pâtés and Terrines' – highly recommended for those who wish to delve further into the subject. This interesting coarse pâté with hazelnuts is best served on hot toast.

450 g/1 lb pig's liver
350 g/12 oz unsalted belly
   pork
225 g/8 oz lard
salt and pepper

small garlic clove
3 tbsp water
3 tbsp Calvados or whisky
100 g/4 oz shelled hazelnuts
pork fat

The large quantity of fat in this recipe is intentional. When baked with less fat, both the flavour and texture of the finished dish are spoiled. Ask the butcher to finely chop the pig's liver and pork belly. If your butcher is unhelpful, then put it through the mincer (coarse plates) when you get it home.

Mix the chopped liver and chopped pork belly with the lard, some salt, pepper, a small peeled garlic clove, the water and Calvados (this is distilled in Normandy from cider apples, but whisky can be used instead when it is unavailable). Now add the shelled unsalted hazelnuts (from health stores and good grocers). Let the mixture stand for an hour before packing it into a big earthenware pot. Cover the top with a piece of fat pork or caul fat, then foil. Bake it in a slow oven 150C/300F/gas 2 for 2½-3 hours.

Let the pâté get cold before putting it away in the refrigerator. It should not really be eaten for two or three days after it has been cooked.

PAPRIKÁSPASTÉTOM

A creamy meat dish with a light flavour, excellent as a first course, particularly with rye bread.

675 g/1½ lb pie veal, diced and trimmed	1 tbsp tomato purée
1 medium onion	6 egg yolks
100 g/4 oz butter	paprika
50 g/2 oz lard	½ tsp salt
	2 tbsp water

Peel and dice the onion finely, heat lard in a large frying pan and cook the onion gently till soft and golden. Stir in 2 teaspoons of paprika and add pie veal. Roll it in the melted lard and paprika. Add the salt and a couple of tablespoons of water, then put a lid on the pan and let it simmer gently, stirring from time to time and adding a very little water occasionally. There should never be a lot of liquid.

After 30 minutes stir in tomato purée. When the meat is tender, let it cool and put the whole thing, meat and gravy through the mincer, fine plates. Then, having beaten egg yolks and softened butter together till smooth and creamy, mix this roughly with the cold minced meat. Pack the mixture into a suitable terrine.

Rillettes are a variation on pâté, very popular with many people but not to the taste of others. They are delicious bits of meat, slowly roasted to remove all fat. However, after the meat is shredded, the fat is used as a binding agent. Provided the high fat content doesn't phase you, the flavour of the rillettes is well worth a try.

900 g/2 lb belly pork	¼ tsp ground nutmeg
3 tbsp dry white wine	pinch ground allspice
2 tsp peppercorns, crushed	pinch ground cloves
¼ tsp salt	1 large clove garlic, crushed

Remove rind and bones and chop meat into small pieces. Add wine, spices, garlic and salt and pepper. Cover and bake 1½-2 hours at 120C/250F/gas ½.

Strain the meat, reserving the fat. Pull the meat into shreds with two forks. When it has cooled, press into glass or earthenware dish, and pour on a layer of the reserved fat.

Leave to set before serving.

RILETTES (2)

900 g/2 lb belly of pork
350 g/12 oz pork fat, chopped
salt and pepper
1 clove garlic, crushed

1 bay leaf
½ tsp parsley
½ tsp rosemary or thyme
150 ml/¼ pint water

Remove rind and bones from the belly of pork, and cut meat into small pieces. Combine meat, fat, salt and pepper and garlic. Put into oven-proof dish and sprinkle over herbs and water. Cover and bake 4 hours at 140C/275F/gas 1, stirring occasionally.

Strain the meat, reserving the fat. Pull the meat into shreds with two forks. When it has cooled, press into glass or earthenware dish, and cover with a layer of the reserved fat.

Leave to set before serving.

CHICKEN PÂTÉ

A light, attractive blend of pork, veal and poultry. Well seasoned, with a combination of minced and whole meats, turkey can be substituted for chicken with great success.

225 g/8 oz lean pork
225 g/8 oz pork fat
225 g/8 oz pie veal
225 g/8 oz cooked ham
225 g/8 oz chicken breast
900 g/2 lb chicken meat

salt and pepper
1 tbsp mixed herbs
50 ml/2 fl oz brandy
2 large eggs, beaten
thin slices of pork fat

Line baking pan with thin slices of fat. Slice breast meat thinly.

Mince all meats together, except for chicken breast. Add salt and pepper, herbs, brandy and eggs. Mix well.

Spread half of meat mixture over fat in pan. Arrange slices of breast on top and cover with remaining minced meat. Place a few more slices of pork fat over the top.

Cover the pan with foil, place in a larger pan with enough hot water to go halfway up sides of pâté dish. Bake 2-3 hours at 150C/300F/gas 2. Place a weight on top of the dish while cooking.

Chill thoroughly before serving.

DUCK PÂTÉ

Delicate orange flavour, with chunks of meat mixing nicely with minced meats.

900 g/2 lb cooked duck meat	½ tsp parsley
1 duck liver	grated rind of 1 orange
225 g/8 oz pie veal	1 egg, beaten
225 g/8 oz belly pork	50 ml/2 fl oz Grand Marnier, brandy or dry sherry
salt and pepper	thin slices pork fat

Thinly slice half of cooked duck meat and set aside.

Mince remaining duck meat with liver, veal and pork. Season, add eggs, orange rind and liquor. Mix well.

Spread half of minced meat mixture over bottom of baking pan. Arrange slices of duck meat on top and cover with remaining minced meat. Place pork fat over the top. Cover the pan with foil, place in a larger pan with enough hot water to go halfway up sides of pâté dish. Bake 1¼ hours at 180C/350F/gas 4.

Chill before serving.

GAME PÂTÉ (1)

Depending on your taste for strongly flavoured dishes and the weight of your purse, these recipes can be used with pigeon, pheasant, wild duck or any other game bird available, individually or in combination. An optional variation which can be used to dress up pigeon pâté is the addition of 50 g/2 oz of chopped walnuts. Both pâtés are very coarse and meaty. The second recipe gives a juicy pâté with a delicious gelatin surrounding it.

225 g/8 oz cooked game	salt and pepper
225 g/8 oz pie veal	2 tbsp juniper berries, crushed
225 g/8 oz pork fat	½ tsp parsley
2 eggs, beaten	pinch ground mace
4 tbsp brandy	½ tsp thyme

Finely chop the pork fat and game. Mince the veal and combine with the chopped meats, seasoning, eggs and brandy. Mix well. Turn into baking pan. Cover with foil, place in a larger pan with enough hot water to go halfway up sides of pâté dish. Bake 1½ hours at 150C/300F/gas 2.

Chill before serving.

GAME PÂTÉ (2)

275 g/10 oz cooked game
225 g/8 oz pie veal
225 g/8 oz belly pork
50 g/2 oz salt pork, pork fat or lard
100 ml/4 fl oz white wine

salt and pepper
2 tsp juniper berries, crushed
1 clove garlic, crushed
thin slices salt pork

Finely chop game and fat. Mince pork and veal. Combine meats, add wine and seasoning. Mix well. Turn into baking dish and arrange slices of salt pork on top.

Cover the pan with foil, place in a larger pan with enough hot water to go halfway up sides of pâté dish. Bake 1¼ hours at 180C/350F/gas 4.

Chill before serving.

RABBIT PÂTÉ

A very strongly flavoured pâté for rabbit fanciers only. The ingredients blend nicely though the rabbit itself predominates.

1.25 kg/2½ lb rabbit meat	1 tbsp thyme
900 g/2 lb belly pork	2 eggs, beaten
225 g/8 oz veal	2 tbsp plain flour
450 g/1 lb onions, chopped	300 ml/½ pint white wine
1 clove garlic, crushed	50 ml/2 fl oz brandy
salt and pepper	thin slices salt pork

Mince the rabbit meat, pork and veal. Add onions, seasoning, wine, brandy, flour and eggs. Mix well. Leave overnight to let flavours mingle.

Arrange slices of salt pork in the bottom of the baking pan.

Turn pâté mixture into pan and arrange slices of salt pork on top. Cover the pan with foil, place in a larger pan with enough hot water to go halfway up sides of pâté dish. Bake 3 hours at 160C/325F/gas 3.

Chill before serving.

SMOKED MACKEREL PÂTÉ

Very quick and easy to make, the cream and fish combine to give a smooth, mild dish, equally suited to lunch or dinner, as a first or main salad course.

350 g/12 oz smoked mackerel,
   skinned and boned
175 g/6 oz butter, melted
100 ml/4 fl oz double cream

3 tbsp lemon juice
salt and pepper
pinch cayenne

Put mackerel into liquidiser and blend with just enough butter to make it smooth. Turn into bowl and gradually add remaining butter, cream, lemon juice and seasoning. Put into serving dish, sprinkle with cayenne and chill.

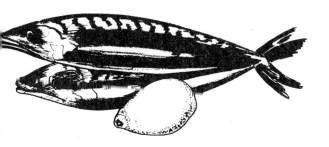

SMOKED SALMON PÂTÉ

An excellent way to stretch a very expensive ingredient into a rich and elegant hors d'oeuvre.

75 g/3 oz cream cheese
grated rind of ½ lemon
1 egg yolk
150 ml/¼ pint single cream
½ small clove garlic,
   crushed

½ tsp salt
black pepper
75 g/3 oz smoked salmon,
   cut into small pieces
3 tbsp chopped parsley
25 g/1 oz white bread

Heat cheese, lemon rind, egg yolk and cream in a small bowl in a pan of hot, but not boiling, water, until smooth and thick.

Put salmon pieces, garlic, salt and pepper, parsley and bread into liquidiser. Add cheese mixture. Blend until smooth, turn into serving dish and chill well.

KIPPER PÂTÉ

Two versions of this ever popular dish. The first is somewhat richer – in taste and pocket – than the second. Both would grace a dinner party and set it going on the right path.

225 g/8 oz kipper fillets,
  skinned and boned
1 tbsp butter, melted
2 tbsp lemon juice
2 tbsp whisky

2 tbsp double cream
dash Worcestershire sauce
dash Tabasco sauce
pepper

Dot kippers with butter and cook in oven in covered dish, 20 minutes at 180C/350F/gas 4. Cool slightly then remove skin and bones.

Put kippers, butter, whisky and lemon juice in liquidiser. Blend until smooth. Add cream and seasoning, mixing well. Put in serving dish and chill.

OR

150 g/5 oz kipper fillets,
  skinned and boned
2 tbsp lemon juice
75 g/3 oz butter, softened

1 tbsp parsley
2 tsp tomato purée
pinch ground mace
pepper

Dot kippers with butter and cook in covered dish, 20 minutes at 180C/350F/gas 4. Cool slightly then remove skin and bones.

Put kippers and lemon juice into liquidiser and blend until smooth. Add to softened butter, tomato purée, parsley and seasoning. Mix well. Chill before serving.

TARAMASALATA

This inexpensive speciality of Greece and Turkey is particularly good with pitta bread and a cucumber-yoghurt salad.

75 g/3 oz tin smoked
  cod's roe
50 g/2 oz white bread
milk to soak

1 clove garlic, crushed
pinch cayenne
3-6 tbsp lemon juice
2-4 tbsp oil

Remove crusts from bread and soak in milk until soft. Squeeze dry, reserving liquid.

Combine cod's roe, bread, garlic and cayenne in electric mixer until smooth. Slowly add lemon juice and oil, tasting frequently. Add milk from soaked bread if a smoother consistency is required.

Chill before serving.

CHOPPED HERRING

A simple and delicious way to dress up rollmops. Very light and an interesting change either as a starter or with a salad for lunch.

4 rollmops, with onions
2 hardboiled eggs
1 cooking apple

1 tbsp matzoh meal (or fine breadcrumbs)

Skin rollmops, and chop with the onions, eggs and apple. Mix in the matzoh meal or breadcrumbs, turn into serving dish and chill.

SMOKED AUBERGINE PÂTÉ

Sharp, smoky flavour makes this a vegetable dish of character.

1 medium aubergine	3-4 tbsp lemon juice
4 hardboiled eggs	2-3 tbsp oil
1 medium Spanish onion	salt and pepper

Place aubergine directly on cooker burner. Cook, turning occasionally, until charred all over. Cool and skin.

Chop aubergine with eggs and onion. Add lemon juice and oil slowly, tasting as you go. Season and chill.